Tugs in Camera

by

Dominic and Bernard McCall

Over the years and especially since the 1960s, the port of Fowey has required a small fleet of tugs to handle ships within its confined waters. On 15 April 2003, two of its tugs, both almost forty years old, were awaiting their next job. The *Tregeagle* was launched on 12 February 1964 at the yard of John Lewis & Sons in Aberdeen. She was delivered on 25 March to the Clyde Shipping Company as *Flying Demon* and became *Forth* when transferred to Forth Tugs Ltd in 1984. She was sold to the Fowey Harbour Commissioners and renamed *Tregeagle* two years later. Power comes from a 6-cylinder British Polar engine of 1015bhp geared to a controllable pitch propeller in a steerable Kort nozzle, giving her a bollard pull of 15 tonnes. In 2013, she was reported to have been sold to an owner in Greencastle, County Donegal, without change of name. Just 16 days after the *Tregeagle* was launched, the keel of the *Pendennick* was laid down at the Hessle yard of Richard Dunston. She was launched on 9 July 1964 and delivered on 17 November to France, Fenwick Tyne & Wear Co Ltd for work at Sunderland as *Dunelm*. She was bought by Fowey Harbour Commissioners and renamed *Pendennick* in 1988. She is driven by an 8-cylinder Ruston & Hornsby engine of 1050bhp geared to a fixed pitch propeller. Between 2009 and 2011 she was noted in various ports including Lowestoft, Great Yarmouth and Blyth. By 2012 she was in Sweden and is understood to have been sold once again in Spring 2014.

(BMc)

Introduction

Many people are interested in ships generally and many are interested in specific types of ships such as warships or cruise vessels. Tugs, too, have an enthusiastic following and many modellers are also keen on these vessels. In this book, we have taken the unusual decision to present a set of images mainly in portrait format rather than the landscape format of most pictorial albums. It seemed to us that tugs in particular lent themselves to this format for aesthetic reasons. The use of this format has enabled us to show close up details which are welcomed by modellers.

It was difficult to decide how much technical information to provide in our captions. We have tended to restrict ourselves to basic information about engines and propulsion units along with bollard pull. The latter measure of towing power has become an increasingly important feature of towage in recent years. Ships being handled have increased in size whilst simple economics would require tug owners to use the minimum number of their vessels on any task. Each tug therefore needs to be of optimum towing capability.

We realise that not all readers will be familiar with names such as Z-peller, Kort nozzle etc. We have made no attempt to explain these, preferring to allow readers to research whatever is necessary.

We should make it clear that not all towage involves shiphandling. Tugs are used for other towage tasks involving barges and cranes and other floating equipment. They are also used to support a wide range of civil engineering projects. Although shiphandling predominates in the pages that follow, we hope that we have given adequate coverage to other types of tugs.

We have made huge efforts to ensure that all the information given is correct. We are very much aware that a considerable quantity of misinformation is available on the internet and errors are now being repeated without question. We have checked and double-checked most of the details given and we apologise if any errors are found. We would like to be told of any such errors.

Throughout its history, the towage industry has seen constant takeovers and mergers amongst the owning companies. In that respect it is like any other industry. Rather than constantly repeat in captions the details of the main changes in UK towage over the last 25 years, we note them here.

By 1990, UK towage had come to be dominated by two companies, the Alexandra Towing Company Ltd and Cory Towage, both having subsumed smaller companies in their recent history. In 1993, Alexandra was taken over by Howard Smith Towage, an Australian company, and in 2001 another Australian company, Adsteam, took over Howard Smith. Meanwhile, in January 2000, it was announced that Cory Towage had been acquired by Wijsmuller Groep Holding, a Dutch company. Only 18 months later, Wijsmuller was itself taken over by Svitzer, a Danish company and part of the huge A P Møller group. In 2006 the inevitable happened when Svitzer made a takeover bid for Adsteam. That was one step too far for the regulatory authorities. The Competition Commission insisted that the Adsteam fleet on the River Mersey had to be sold to a different company. It was acquired by Smit International, based in the Netherlands, and was this company's first entry into harbour towage in the UK.

Acknowledgements

We are extremely grateful to all those who have shared their knowledge with us, especially Chris Jones, Kevin Jones and Danny Lynch. Many individuals, too numerous to name individually, have answered specific questions relating to a particular vessel. Some websites have proved useful, notably Tugtalk and Clyde Maritime. We have referred to several books and Bill Harvey's *Cory Towage*, published by the World Ship Society, has been an excellent source of information. We are also grateful to those who have contributed photographs which are credited individually. As always, many thanks to Gil Mayes for his reading of the initial drafts and wise corrections, and to the staff of Amadeus Press for their superb printing.

Bernard and Dominic McCall,

Portishead, December 2014

Published by Bernard McCall, 400 Nore Road, Portishead, Bristol, BS20 8EZ, England.
Website : www.coastalshipping.co.uk.   Telephone/fax : 01275 846178. Email : bernard@coastalshipping.co.uk.
All distribution enquiries should be addressed to the publisher.

Printed by The Amadeus Press, Ezra House, 26 West Business Park, Cleckheaton, BD19 4TQ.
Telephone : 01274 863210.   Fax: 01274 863211.
Email: info@amadeuspress.co.uk   Website : www.amadeuspress.co.uk.

ISBN : 978-1-902953-67-0

Front cover : Readers will surely notice that many of the modern vessels featured in this book were built by Damen in the Netherlands. For over twenty years the Damen company has had hulls built in other yards and then kept them in reserve until ordered by a customer. One such example is the **Portgarth**. The hull of this tug was built at the SevMash shipyard in Severodvinsk and launched on 3 November 1993. It was then towed to the Damen yard at Gorinchem to await a buyer. This proved to be Cory Towage Ltd and the tug was completed on 30 March 1995. An example of the ASD Tug 3110 design, the **Portgarth** has the distinction of being the first standard shiphandling tug delivered to a British company by Damen. She is driven by two Kromhout engines with a total power of 3980bhp and these are geared to two stern-mounted Z-peller units. It was always intended that she would be based at Avonmouth and Royal Portbury Dock but she has spent periods in other ports such as Milford Haven. She was photographed off Battery Point at Portishead on a sunny but cold 17 January 2004.

(DMc)

Back cover : Ordered from Tille Scheepsbouw, Koostertille, by Goedkoop Havensleepdiensten – Amsterdam, which shortly after became a subsidiary of Wijsmuller, the **Groningen** was the first of four sister vessels. She was launched in November 1980 and delivered on 20 February 1981. Her two 8-cylinder Bolnes engines with a total of 2400bhp drive two Niigata Z-pellers achieving a bollard pull of 30 tonnes. In 1986 engine output was increased to 3060bhp, and a 42 tonne bollard pull was achieved. In that same year she began a two-year charter to "Intercor" at Puerto Bolivar in Colombia. From her return until 2005, the style of her owning company changed frequently as she was transferred within Wijsmuller subsidiary companies. In March 1999 she was fitted with fire-fighting equipment in readiness to work at a tanker terminal at Point Lisas in Trinidad. She returned in 2000. In mid-2005 she transferred to the Portuguese flag as **Svitzer Leixoes** after Svitzer had moved her to its Portuguese subsidiary to work in Lisbon. The photograph was taken at IJmuiden on 4 August 2003 as she assisted the **Cape Falcon** out of the locks and into the North Sea Canal.

(DMc)

The **Agama** was one of nine sister vessels built for the Royal Maritime Auxiliary Service (RMAS) and known as the Improved Girl class. She was built as **Dorothy** at the Richard Dunston shipyard in Thorne and was based in Hong Kong after delivery in 1969. It was in July 1978 that she returned to Portsmouth. She left RMAS service in 1991 when bought by Alan C Bennett & Sons, based at Rochester. She was needed to assist with work on the Limehouse relief road project. Renamed **Agama**, she was bought two years later by Maldon-based Nigel Cardy and she was photographed at that Essex port in August 2005. Power comes from a 6-cylinder Lister-Blackstone engine of 495bhp and she has a bollard pull of 6 tonnes.

(BMc)

The **Flying Fulmar** had a rather problematic start. Launched at the Wallsend yard of Ryton Marine on 2 July 1973, completion was delayed because of the financial collapse of the building company and she was not delivered to Clyde Shipping until early February 1974. Power came from two 6-cylinder British Polar engines each of 1201bhp and geared to a controllable pitch propeller. This achieved a bollard pull of 37 tonnes. We see her outward bound in the Firth of Clyde on 24 July 1978. In mid-1992 she was sold to Palermo-based owners and on her delivery voyage towed fleetmate **Flying Scout** that had been bought by the same owners. She was renamed **Alce Nero** by her new Italian owners.

(BMc)

The **Warrior III** is a much-travelled tug. She was built by Kanagawa Zosen at Kobe for Japanese owners and was delivered as **Hayakuni Maru** on 10 June 1975. Power comes from two 6-cylinder Niigata engines totalling 2600bhp and driving twin stern-mounted Z-peller units. This combination gives her a bollard pull of 37 tonnes. In 1990 she was sold to owners in Setubal and hoisted the Portuguese flag as **Montenovo**. Three years later, she was acquired by Celtic Tugs Ltd and renamed **Celtic Warrior**. In mid-February 1996 she was bought by Cory Towage, renamed **Warrior**, and was immediately used in the salvage of the **Sea Empress** which had grounded at Milford Haven.

Once this work had been completed she was returned to Cork for rebuilding. After completion she transferred to the UK flag as **Warrior III**, the name **Warrior** being already registered. She was based on the Clyde and we see her approaching James Watt Dock at Greenock on 25 July 2004 with Greenock Ocean Terminal in the distance. She moved to Milford Haven in 2010 but by 2013 she was laid up in Avonmouth. Renamed **Christos XXV** on 13 August 2013, she left Avonmouth the next day for Piraeus towed by **Pantodynamos**.

(DMc)

In the early 1970s, there was a rapid growth in exploration for oil beneath the North Sea. Once the crude oil was pumped ashore, new terminals were needed to export the oil and one of these terminals was at Sullom Voe in the Shetland Islands. In anticipation of meeting the towage requirements, Shetland Towage Ltd was established in 1975, this being a partnership between the Shetland Islands Council (50%), Clyde Shipping Company (25%) and Cory Towage (25%). Construction began in 1975 and the first oil came ashore in late 1978. Three tugs were purpose-built and we see one of these on the next page. By the time that the terminal was completed in 1981 it was clear that more tugs were needed and two Voith-Schneider tractor tugs were ordered from Ferguson Bros at Port Glasgow. These are named *Tirrick* and *Shalder* after Shetland seabirds and are powered by two 12-cylinder Ruston engines totalling 4000bhp and geared to two Voith-Schneider propulsion units; they have a bollard pull of 45 tonnes. The *Tirrick* was the first to be launched, this taking place on 1 February 1983 with the *Shalder* following on 30 March. The respective delivery dates were 17 June 1983 and 15 August 1983. The construction of two new replacement tugs in Spain was delayed and, when they did arrive in 2011, there were problems that continued until 2014 and this has enabled the *Tirrick* and *Shalder*, photographed on 24 February 2005, to remain in use longer than expected.

(DMc)

The third of three sisterships, the **Battleaxe** was launched at the Hall, Russell shipyard in Aberdeen on 5 July 1978 and delivered as **Lyrie** to Shetland Towage on 6 November. Power comes from two 12-cylinder Ruston engines, each of 1899bhp, geared to two controllable pitch propellers in steerable Kort nozzles, a combination giving her a bollard pull of 54 tonnes. In 1996, she was renamed **Elsie** and, with sister tug **Evelynn**, was refitted on the River Tyne for a contract at an oil terminal at Puerto Armuelles on the Pacific coast of Panama. As the tugs were passing through the Panama Canal, news came that the contract had been cancelled and both tugs were laid up at Willemstad. They were reactivated in June 1997, and again modified and refurbished, to service a new but relatively short Cory contract at the oil terminal at St Eustatius in the Netherlands Antilles. The **Elsie** returned to the UK and arrived at Greenock on 9 September 1998. In March 1999 she was sent to Lithuania to work on a contract to provide towage services at the Butinge single point mooring of Mazeikiu Nafta, the Lithuanian state-owned oil company. In spring 2007 she moved to Cape Town and by summer 2014 this much-travelled tug was assisting tankers at Lagos. We see her approaching Port Talbot on 6 September 2005.

(DMc)

The **Forager** was an unusual vessel to appear in the Cory fleet. She was built at the Damen shipyard in Hardinxveld in 1988 and was completed as **Frances** for Holyhead Towing Co Ltd but was subsequently renamed **Afon Wen**. She was acquired by Cory Towage in March 1999 after Cory had won the two-year contract to provide services at the Butinge single point mooring. As a tug/workboat, she was deemed ideal to support the **Battleaxe** which had arrived at the terminal on 6 March. The **Afon Wen** was renamed **Forager** in May 1999 and was registered in Klaipeda under the Lithuanian flag. She is powered by two 8-cylinder Caterpillar engines geared to twin fixed pitch propellers within steerable Kort nozzles. She has a modest bollard pull of 13 tonnes. Having been acquired for a specific contract, it was not easy to know where to place her on completion of that contract but she was deemed too useful to be sold. In 2005 she was sent to the Bristol Channel mainly to provide escort services for larger vessels navigating the River Avon to Bristol City Docks, following a decision that all such vessels were to have a tug escort. We see her in the Cumberland Basin in July 2005. By 2007 she had moved to work at the Lindø shipyard near Odense and she has remained a useful vessel there.

(BMc)

The **Flying Spindrift** was launched at the Richard Dunston shipyard in Hessle on 28 October 1985 and delivered to the Clyde Shipping Company on 31 January 1986. She is driven by two Ruston engines, each of 1550bhp geared to two stern-mounted Aquamaster units incorporating a Kort nozzle. This gives her a bollard pull of 38 tonnes. Her design was significant for several reasons. The wheelhouse, intended for operation by one person, has a foot-operated radio switch to enable full communication even when the master may be otherwise fully occupied. Although novel at the time, such equipment is now standard in modern tugs. Thanks to the absence of funnels and uptakes, all-round vision is excellent. In 1994 she was transferred to Lawson-Batey Tugs, Newcastle, and in May of the following year was taken over by Cory Towage. She passed through the ownership of Wijsmuller and Svitzer, the latter transferring her to its Felixarc Marine subsidiary in 2009. In June 2012 she was sold to Farsund Fortøyningsselskap, Farsund, Norway and renamed **FFS Atlas** under the St Vincent & Grenadines flag. She left Lowestoft for Farsund on 30 June 2012. We see her assisting the **Chun Ho** into the lock at Cardiff on 26 April 2007.

(Kevin Jones)

Towage within the port of Antwerp is carried out by the Antwerp Port Authority's own tugs which have a tradition of being numbered rather than named. Built by the local SKB Shipyard for the Port Authority in 2002, **22** is the third of three sisters and is seen assisting the **MSC Lieselotte** in Antwerp on 2 June 2005. A pair of ABC diesels drive two forward-mounted Voith-Schneider propulsion units. This gives the tugs a bollard pull of 55 tonnes and speed of 13.5 knots. The three tugs are based on earlier tugs in the authority's fleet delivered in 1999 and retain the dimensions of 29,50m x 11,00m and much of the layout of the earlier vessels, but they have increased horsepower and bollard pull, along with the addition of the mast mounted above the wheelhouse. A further difference is the addition of an extra winch on the aft deck in place of a towing hook.

(DMc)

The hull of the **Schelde 10** was built by HH Bodewes at Millingen a/d Rijn but she was completed by Scheepswerf en Gashouderbouw v/h Jonker & Stans at Hendrik Ido Ambacht. Although launched in 1984, she was not delivered to Antwerp-based owners Schelde Towage until May 1987. Power comes from two 6-cylinder MWM engines with a total output of 2447bhp geared to two fixed pitch propellers in Kort nozzles. This gives her a bollard pull of 32 tonnes. When Unie van Redding Sleepdienst (URS) took over Schelde Towage in 2000 she moved to that fleet and then entered the Smit fleet in 2010 when Smit took over URS. Smit soon transferred her from the Belgian flag to that of Liberia and she was deleted from the Belgian register on 21 December 2010. Along with sister tug **Schelde 12**, she was assigned to work for Smit Terminals in the port of Monrovia where she arrived in January 2011. In April 2013 she was sold to another Smit subsidiary, Smit Lamnalco Netherlands BV, and was renamed **SL Schelde**. The photograph was taken on 2 June 2005 as she approached the lock at Antwerp. *(DMc)*

The construction of the tunnel under the English Channel was a huge civil engineering task. In England a consortium of builders and banks was formed and the same happened in France. These two consortia then merged under the title TransManche Link (TML) and it was this company that ordered the **Shakespeare**, a Delta Tug 1450 vessel, from Delta Shipyards in Sliedrecht. She was delivered in 1988 as **Rachel** but was soon renamed as she worked at the Shakespeare Cliff site. Her role was to assist the floating craft that were used to construct and maintain artificial lagoons which contained spoil from boring operations. Once her work for TML was completed she was bought by Maritime Craft Services for whom she proved to be an excellent vessel. During the summer of 2006 she was contracted to assist with dredging at Aberdeen as seen here. She was sold on to Piraeus-based Atlantic Dredging in 2007 and, now named **Aiolos**, supports this company's work off the coast of Africa. She is driven by two Caterpillar engines totalling 760bhp geared to fixed-pitch propellers in Kort nozzles and giving her a bollard pull of 8 tonnes.

(DMc)

It is pleasing to be able to include an image of a relatively modern tug built at a shipyard in the UK. The **Prince Rock** was built for the Cattewater Harbour Commissioners by VT Halmatic at Portchester. This company had been formed in 1998 when Vosper Thornycroft took over Halmatic, hitherto a builder of specialist military craft. A complex series of company changes saw Halmatic relocate to Portsmouth Naval Base as a legacy brand of BAE Systems. The **Prince Rock** exemplifies the Halmatic WB 18 design, the other three examples of this design being built for Russian ownership. Power comes from two 6-cylinder Cummins engines, each of 700bhp and geared to two fixed pitch propellers in fixed Kort nozzles. This arrangement gives her a bollard pull of 18 tonnes. She is seen at Plymouth on 15 October 2005.

(DMc)

We now look at two tugs constructed in the mid-1930s. The ***Crested Cock*** was built by Alexander Hall & Co Ltd in Aberdeen. She was powered by a 3-cylinder steam engine of 1000 ihp. She was launched on 5 March 1935 and delivered the following month to Gamecock Steam Towing Co Ltd in Gravesend. On 31 May 1940 she towed a lighter across the English Channel to Dunkirk and returned immediately to Dover. She returned to Dunkirk the next day and was engaged in assisting small craft. By 12 June she had returned to the Thames. During 1941 she assisted in the building of the Maunsell anti-aircraft forts in the Thames estuary. On 1 February 1950, her owning company amalgamated with two others to form Ship Towage (London) Ltd but the tugs of the constituent companies retained their own colours until 1965. We see the ***Crested Cock*** in the River Thames during August 1968 quite late in her career. On 27 January 1969 she became part of the fleet of London Tugs Ltd but this was only brief as she arrived for demolition at Willebroek in Belgium in late February 1970.

(John Wiltshire)

The ***John King*** is a steel-hulled tug built by Charles Hill & Sons Ltd, Bristol, for C J King & Sons on the lines of a steam tug. Launched on 21 October 1935, she was delivered in February of the following year. She was used for ship towage on the River Avon and in Bristol Docks until 1970. During the blitz of 1940, she was employed for seventeen days fighting fires at the Pembroke Dock oil installations and, on her way back to Bristol, was attacked by a German aircraft. Her last job in King ownership, on 6 July 1970, was to escort the ***Great Britain*** into the Great Western Dock. She was purchased in 1970 by F A Ashmead & Son for further service on the Severn and renamed ***Peter Leigh***. Her work involved towing African hardwood logs in barges from Avonmouth across the River Severn to Lydney. In 1978, she was sold to Bristol Commercial Ships and renamed ***Pride***, and worked as far as Southampton and Milford Haven. In 1986 she took the name ***Durdham***. In 1988 she had engine trouble off the Devon coast whilst towing and was herself towed into Salcombe. In 1995, she was purchased by the Bristol Industrial Museum and reverted to her original name. She has been kept in working condition and is part of the new Museum of Bristol. In July 2001 she was used to assist the coaster ***Lucie*** during the performances of the play "Up the Feeder, Down the 'Mouth, and Back Again" which was being performed in the former industrial museum behind the tug.

(BMc)

The **Argonaut** was built at Millingen by Scheepswerven v/h H. H. Bodewes and was delivered to L Smit & Co on 11 July 1963. The title of the owning company changed over the years as the Smit company expanded. In 1989 she was bought by Rochester-based Alan C Bennett & Partners and was renamed **Argonaut B**, reverting to **Argonaut** some eleven years later. Power came from a 7-cylinder De Industrie engine which gave her a bollard pull of 13 tonnes. In 2011 she was laid up at Coldharbour Jetty on the River Thames and was demolished two years later. We see her assisting the arrival of the **Aurora Jade** at Northfleet on the River Thames on 18 March 1995.

(Ian Willett)

The **Cobham** was a product of the McTay shipyard at Bromborough where she was launched for the Dover Harbour Board as **Dextrous** on 17 April 1984. A notable feature was that her fendering system, especially at the stern, had been designed to assist in the berthing of large cross-channel ferries. Power comes from two 6-cylinder Ruston engines, each of 1336bhp and geared to two Voith-Schneider propellers. This gives her a bollard pull of 29 tonnes. She became **Cobham** in 2000 after being acquired by Howard Smith Towage but ownership was transferred to Adsteam in the following year and we see her in Adsteam colours in the lock at Tilbury on 26 October 2003. Some

three years later, she was transferred to the Humber Tugs fleet (see page 62). It was in spring 2007 that Svitzer took over Adsteam and she became **HT Cutlass**. She was later transferred to South Wales with occasional visits to the English side of the Bristol Channel. Not powerful enough for much of the work required, she was eventually sold in 2013 to Zulia Towing & Barge Co, of Maracaibo, and left Avonmouth on 17 July 2013 on board the heavy-lift ship **HHL Venice** bound for Venezuela.

(DMc)

The **Canada** was another tug from the McTay shipyard in Bromborough. Built for Alexandra Towing, she was launched on 25 October 1980 and delivered during December. She was one of the first shiphandling tugs fitted with Voith-Schneider propulsion built for a UK tug operator. The tug was built for Alexandra's Liverpool fleet and was thus named after the famous Canada Dock of Liverpool's dock system, replacing the 1960-built **Canada** that worked as **Pea Cock** until 1970 (see page 53). Ownership passed to Howard Smith and then Adsteam Towage. A condition of the Svitzer takeover of Adsteam was that the latter's Mersey operation should be taken over by a different company and thus Smit entered the UK harbour towage business. The **Canada** became **Smit Canada** but in 2008 she was sold to TP Towage of Gibraltar to supplement their existing fleet of former Howard Smith tugs and renamed **Wellington**. To achieve her bollard pull of 32 tonnes she is fitted with two Ruston 6-cylinder engines which produce 2640bhp and give a speed of 12 knots. We see her assisting a vessel in the Birkenhead dock system in March 1992.

(BMc)

In 1990, the Howard Smith Group awarded to McTay Marine the highest value tug order ever placed in the UK. Valued at £15 million, it was for five tugs to operate on the Humber. They were to be of a radical new design with the bridge placed centrally thus allowing easier maintenance of the Voith propulsion units and also offering better stability. The wheelhouse was designed to allow maximum all-round vision and great use was made of overhead panels for instrumentation and control. Construction of the hull sections was contracted out and these were delivered to the shipyard by road. The **Lady Anya** was the first to be delivered and she was followed on 30 January 1991 by the **Lady Kathleen** which had been launched on 15 November 1990. She is powered by two 6-cylinder Ruston engines, each of 2366bhp and geared to two Voith-Schneider propulsion units. This gives her a bollard pull of 53 tonnes. She is a very manoeuvrable vessel. The takeovers mentioned in the introduction saw her become **Adsteam Kathleen** in 2006 and **Svitzer Kathleen** in the following year. We see her off Immingham in July 2004.

(DMc)

The **Uskgarth** was the third of five similar tugs built for R & J H Rea by Richards (Shipbuilders) Ltd at Lowestoft, all five being intended for use on the Bristol Channel. The first of the five, **Lowgarth**, was to be an evaluation vessel but such was the urgent need for tugs in the Bristol Channel at the time that the evaluation was not fully completed and the four tugs that followed were built merely with different engines although the last one in the series, **Bargarth**, did have a hull that was modified during construction. The **Uskgarth** was launched on 9 December 1965 and delivered on 11 March 1966. Although ownership was transferred to Cory in 1970, it was not until 1985 that she gained Cory funnel colours. Power comes from an 8-cylinder Blackstone engine geared to a fixed pitch propeller within a steerable Kort nozzle. This combination gives her a 14 tonne bollard pull. In November 1995, the tug was reported as sold to owners at Port Louis in Mauritius and was soon renamed **Tamar** under the flag of Belize. We see her on 23 July 1989 as she was about to enter the passage between No. 2 Dock and No. 1 Dock in Barry acting as stern tug to a large vessel inward bound with a cargo of timber.

(BMc)

The **Hallgarth**, and sistership **Holmgarth**, represented a significant development in towage in the UK. The use of multidirectional tugs was well established in other parts of Europe but British tug owners were largely unconvinced. In the late 1970s, however, Cory Towage ordered four such tugs from Scott & Sons at Bowling. The **Holmgarth** was the first to be delivered and she was soon followed by **Hallgarth**, launched on 15 February 1979 and completed on 28 June. Both were based at Cardiff. They have two 6-cylinder Ruston engines, each of 1067bhp, geared to twin Voith-Schneider multidirectional propellers. Each has a bollard pull of 23.5 tons. Whereas sister tug **Holmgarth** saw service elsewhere including Liverpool, Dublin and even Stranraer, the **Hallgarth** rarely left the Bristol Channel. In late 2007 she was laid up at Avonmouth and in spring 2008 was sold to Falmouth Towage by whom she was renamed **St Piran**. Here we see the **Hallgarth** at speed out of No. 1 Dock in Barry after assisting a reefer to the berth on 23 August 1989.

(BMc)

The **Svitzer Muiden** is one of ten similar firefighting tugs whose hulls were constructed at the Western Baltija Shipbuilding yard in Klaipeda with completion by Odense Staalskibsværft at Lindo. The second part of the name of each begins with the letter M and they have become known as the M series. The first four tugs of the series are powered by two medium speed 6-cylinder MAK main engines producing a total of 4890bhp driving a pair of Rolls Royce US205 CP Aquamaster propulsion units. This combination gives them a bollard pull of 62 tons. The **Svitzer Muiden** was the last of these four and arrived at IJmuiden on 20 December 2004. She had just assisted the bulk carrier **Matrix** out of the lock at IJmuiden when photographed on 29 May 2006.

(DMc)

The remaining six tugs in the Svitzer M series have two high speed 16-cylinder Caterpillar main engines each of 2855bhp and again geared to two Rolls-Royce Aquamaster propulsion units. This gives them a bollard pull of 73 tonnes, slightly higher than that of the four earlier tugs. The **Svitzer Marken** was delivered on 6 February 2005 and arrived in her home port of IJmuiden nine days later. In 2009 she was chartered by the Dutch government to serve as standby and emergency towing vessel during the absence of the usual tug in that role. In late December 2013 she left IJmuiden to begin work at Bremerhaven along with sister vessel **Svitzer Mallaig** from the UK. The tugs were to be employed in a joint venture with local operator URAG but the German competition authority was slow to ratify this agreement and had not done so at the time of publication. The first two companies to use the Svitzer tugs at Bremerhaven were Mærsk (not surprising as Svitzer is part of the Møller/Mærsk group) and the Mediterranean Shipping Company. We see her at IJmuiden on 22 June 2006.

(BMc)

The **Libra Star** was launched as **Walborg** at the A van Bennekum shipyard at Sliedrecht on 11 May 1965 and delivered to Dutch owners on 16 July. Her 4-cylinder Brons engine of 240bhp is geared to a single screw and gives her a bollard pull of 5 tonnes. She came into British ownership at the end of March 1983 when purchased by ARC Marine Ltd by whom she was renamed **Arco Deben**. In 1992 she was acquired by Middlesbrough-based River Tees Engineering & Welding Ltd and was given the name **Libra Star**. At the time of writing, the tug remains on the River Tees but is understood to be little used. We see her at Middlesbrough on 15 July 2005. In the background is the Tees Transporter Bridge, officially opened on 17 October 1911 and one of only eight such bridges still surviving in the world and one of only five still in use.

(DMc)

The **Revenge** is a typical Thames lighterage tug. She was built in 1948 at the Richard Dunston shipyard in Thorne and was delivered to Wm Cory Lighterage Ltd. In 1982, ownership was transferred to the Lee and Brentford Lighterage Co Ltd which was offering a link between London's dock system and Brentford, thus avoiding the capital's congested roads. Sadly the venture did not prove successful and the company ceased trading in October 1984, the **Revenge** being its only vessel. She was sold in 1985 to General Marine Ltd. She is driven by a Lister-Blackstone engine of 528bhp which replaced her original Crossley engine of 330 bhp. She has a bollard pull of 5.6 tonnes. Tower Bridge is silhouetted in the background as the **Revenge** pulls away from Tower Pier in May 1996.

(BMc)

The **Clairvoyant** and **Aventureux** were part of a group of four (**Farouche**, and **Triomphant** were the others) delivered for Les Abeilles at Dunkirk in the last half of 1999. Their hulls were built by Alstom Leroux Naval at St Malo with completion at the company's yard in Lorient. A further two very similar tugs were later delivered to Le Havre but had the addition of fire-fighting equipment (**Abeille Antifer** and **Abeille La Hève**). The last two Dunkerque tugs to be delivered also have the capacity to hold 9m³ of recovered oil. The tugs are powered by two 6-cylinder Anglo-Belgian Corporation diesels each of 1767bhp, driving two Rolls-Royce Aquamaster thrusters that are mounted forward of the wheelhouse. A bollard pull of 40.5 tonnes was achieved on trials, and free running speed of 12 knots. An interesting feature of these tugs is the deck area between the towing winch and fairlead where there is a clear area sized to accommodate a 20ft container. We see the two tugs at Dunkirk on 20 September 2006.

(DMc)

Both tugs seen here were delivered new to Cory Towage, the **Anglegarth** being completed and handed over in December 1996 while the **Millgarth** arrived for handing over on 23 February 1997. They were ordered in 1995 following the award of a contract by the Texaco, Gulf Oil, and Elf refineries in Milford Haven. Both tugs are of the Damen ASD 3211 design, but delivered a little later than the Howard Smith trio described on page 63 and were fitted with two Stork – Wärtsilä engines which give a greater bollard pull of 66 tonnes ahead. The hulls for the two tugs were built by Stocznia Polnocna S. A. Northern Yard, in Gdansk, Poland, prior to being towed to the Netherlands for completion. The official naming of the two tugs took place on 14 March 1997 and was carried out by children from local schools. Both vessels have spent most of their working lives in Milford but were displaced to other ports following completion of the new tugs which were built to service new LNG terminals. In mid-2013, the **Anglegarth** was working on the Clyde and **Millgarth** on the Thames but the latter moved to the Mersey in April 2014. Photographed at Milford Haven on 29 May 2003, the tugs carry the Svitzer livery of the time along with the Wijsmuller name on their hull.

(DMc)

Photographed at Leith on the evening of 28 September 1989, the **Boquhan** was named after a village near Stirling and was one of two tugs ordered by Clyde Shipping Ltd from the Robb Caledon shipyard in Leith. She was launched on 14 August 1975 and delivered on 7 January 1976. She and sister tug **Duchray** were designed to work at the newly-opened Hound Point tanker terminal on the southern bank of the Firth of Forth. Power came from a single 12-cylinder Ruston engine of 2640bhp geared to a controllable pitch propeller in a steerable Kort nozzle. This gave her a bollard pull of 38 tonnes. A notable feature was the fire-fighting tower 21.6 metres high. In 1996, BP decided to operate its own tugs at Hound Point and the **Boquhan**, along with the other three tugs in the fleet was taken out of use in December 1996. She was sold in 1997 to be operated as a diving support vessel near Conakry off the coast of West Africa. She left the Firth of Forth on 23 October 1997 and sailed to Hull where a deck crane was fitted. Named **Oliver**, she departed Hull on 5 November. Although renamed **Nano** in 2009, there are no further reports of her whereabouts.

(Ian Willett)

The **Carron**, launched on 30 April 1979, was constructed by Scott & Sons, Bowling, and was the penultimate vessel to be built at this yard, the final one being her sister tug **Forth**, launched on 25 June 1979. Both were purpose-built for operation in Grangemouth Dock by Forth Tugs Ltd, which at the time was owned 50% by Clyde Shipping Co, and 50% Cory Ship Towage Ltd. The tugs were ideal for Grangemouth having firefighting capabilities, and the twin Voith-Schneider propellers were eminently suitable for working in the tight confines of the relatively small locks and dock system of Grangemouth. Each tug had two 6-cylinder Ruston engines providing a total of 2200bhp with a 24 tonne bollard pull. In 2008 **Carron** was sold to Sinbad Marine Services, of Killybegs in the Republic of Ireland but in 2012 returned to the Firth of Forth following purchase by the Forth Crossing Bridge Constructors JV and managed by Briggs Marine. The **Forth** was sold in 2003 and replaced by a tug which took over the name and is seen here. This was the **Cleveland Cross**, launched at the Richard Dunston shipyard in Hessle on 18 September 1989 and delivered on 22 October. She is powered by two 6-cylinder Ruston engines totalling 3382bhp and driving two Voith-Schneider propellers and giving a bollard pull of 37 tonnes. The photograph was taken at Grangemouth on 19 January 2005.

(DMc)

In the mid-1990s, there was some surprise when long-established Belgian tug operator URS (Unie van Redding en Sleepdienst) placed an order for six tugs at the Astilleros Armon shipyard at Navia in Spain. The **Union 11** was one of these tugs. She is powered by two 8-cylinder Deutz engines, each of 2039bhp and geared to two Voith-Schneider propellers. This gives her a bollard pull of 43 tonnes. In 2003, Smit International, which already had a 49.9% share in URS, obtained the remaining 50.1% although it was some considerable time before the changes were reflected in the livery of the tugs. It was not until early 2013 that the **Union 11** appeared in Smit colours and also was seen regularly in Rotterdam. She was photographed at Antwerp on 2 June 2005.

(DMc)

Delivered in June and August 2001 were two sisters **Union Diamond** and **Union Sapphire**. Also built by Astilleros Armon at Navia, both tugs entered service with URS in Antwerp. This order maintained a significant link between URS and Armon as URS was the first international operator to order tugs from the Spanish builder. A pair of 8-cylinder ABC engines, each of 2515bhp, drive a pair of stern-mounted Schottel rudder/propellers and the tugs are also fitted with a Schottel bow thruster. This arrangement gives the tug a bollard pull of 63 tonnes ahead. The tugs are equally suited to harbour work or coastal work, with three twin cabins and three single cabins being provided, along with galley, separate mess, laundry, and office. Seen swinging in the largest locks at Antwerp to proceed back out to her berth on 13 July 2004, the vessel assisted into the locks by the **Union Sapphire** would use towage services from Antwerp Port Authority tugs once inside the dock system.

(DMc)

Following the success of the earlier vessels, URS returned to Astilleros Armon for four anchor-handling tugs. The first of the quartet was the **Union Warrior** which was delivered in November 2009 and entered service in West Africa on an initial three-year charter, mainly to assist tankers loading at the Girassol and Pazflor terminals. This was extended and we see her off the coast of Angola on 29 November 2013 with the drilling rig **Ocean Rig Olympia** in the background. The **Union Warrior** and her sister ships are considerably larger than the **Union Sapphire** and her sisters. The tugs have a high, well-fendered forecastle for maximum protection at sea and are equipped for towing,

anchor-handling and fire-fighting to FiFi 1 standard. Power comes from two 12-cylinder ABC engines each of 3606bhp and geared to two Schottel fully azimuthing propulsion units incorporating fixed pitch propellers. This combination gives her a bollard pull of 85 tonnes. Despite URS having been in Smit ownership for six years, the **Union Warrior** and her sisters were all given traditional URS names, the others being **Union Fighter**, **Union Boxer** and **Union Wrestler**. All were in Smit livery, however, as seen here. It is interesting to note that Smit International itself was taken over by the Royal Boskalis Westminster group just after these four tugs were delivered.

(DMc)

Before returning to the UK, we take a glance at a tug in southern Europe. The Italian towage company Fratelli Neri was established in Livorno in the first decade of the twentieth century. Its founder was Tito Neri, born in 1888, and it has remained a private family-owned company throughout its existence. The **Tito Neri Settimo**, photographed at Livorno in August 1997, was built at Ancona by C. N. Cooperativa Metallurgica G Tommasi. Her main engine is an 8-cylinder Nohab of 2039bhp and this is geared to a fixed pitch propeller in a Kort nozzle, giving her a bollard pull of 30 tonnes. On the night of 10 April 1991, she was one of the first vessels to reach the scene of the tragic collision between the ferry **Moby Prince** and crude oil tanker **AGIP Abruzzo** that was anchored some two miles off the entrance to the port of Livorno. There was only one survivor from the 141 passengers and crew on the ferry. In 2009, the **Tito Neri Settimo** was sold to Greek owners and renamed **Hector**.

(BMc)

The **Yorkshireman** was a product of the Charles D Holmes shipyard in Beverley. She was launched on 12 April 1967 and delivered on 22 June to United Towing in Hull. She was renamed **Lady Theresa** in 1975 and was photographed as such in the Humber in July 1981. Later that year she was sold to well-known Greek tug owner Alexander G Tsavliris and was renamed **Atlas**. She retained her name and Piraeus registry following purchase by Lyboussakis Salvage & Towage in 2002. Her two 6-cylinder Ruston & Hornsby engines, each of 1201bhp, drive two fixed pitch propellers and provide a bollard pull of 36 tonnes according to her owners. Despite approaching her golden jubilee she continues to be used in the Piraeus area.

(BMc)

The first of a four tug order, this **Lady Theresa** was launched at Cochrane's Selby shipyard on 25 September 1987 and delivered to Humber Tugs Ltd on 26 January the following year. We see her fitting out in drydock in Goole in mid-December 1987. Power comes from two 6-cylinder Ruston engines, each of 950bhp and geared to two fixed pitch propellers within fixed Kort nozzles. After only six years service on the Humber she moved north to the River Tyne following purchase by Clyde Shipping Ltd who gave her the traditional local Tyneside name of **Hillsider**. Her time as such was brief for Cory acquired her (and the owning company) in 1995 by which time her bow had been modified. In March 2000, Cory Towage was taken over by Wijsmuller but six months later she was sold to the Fairplay group to work in Rotterdam as **Fairplay XI**. She was later transferred to Fairplay's Polish subsidiary but in December 2013 she returned to German ownership when bought by Hamburg-based Lührs Schiffahrt and renamed **Twister**.

(BMc)

The Royal Maritime Auxiliary Service (RMAS) used to form the major part of the Marine Services organisation which existed to support the Royal Navy. It was a branch of the Ministry of Defence (Naval). Ship towage was one of a wide range of services provided by the RMAS. All RMAS vessels had a buff coloured superstructure and black hulls with an all round white riband at deck level. The *Florence* is one of eight vessels usually called water tractors and used for the handling of barges. She was built at the Richard Dunston shipyard in Hessle but fitted out in Goole where we see her on 22 July 1980 in a different drydock from that used by *Lady Theresa* on the previous page. She was accepted into the RMAS fleet on 8 August 1980. Power comes from a Lister Blackstone engine of 600bhp and she has a bollard pull of 5.8 tonnes. Propulsion comes from a single Voith-Schneider unit and the inclusion of this photograph will hopefully enable readers unfamiliar with such equipment to gain an impression of its appearance. After Serco Denholm, later Serco Marine Services, took over the former RMAS vessels, she was renamed *SD Florence*.

(BMc)

In August 1996 responsibility for running the majority of the RMAS vessels was transferred to Serco Ltd Marine Services under a Government Owned/Commercially Operated (GOCO) contract. From 1 April 2008 Serco Marine Services became the contractor responsible for the operation of all Marine Services vessels in the UK, following the award of the Future Provision of Marine Services (FPMS) contract by MoD. All vessels became commercial vessels and their names were modified with the prefix SD, thus **Faithful** became **SD Faithful**. Another product of the Dunston yard at Hessle, she was accepted into the RMAS on 13 December 1985. She has two Ruston engines geared to twin Voith-Schneider propulsion units and a bollard pull of 26 tonnes. She was photographed at speed in Plymouth Sound on 15 October 2005.

(DMc)

We now look at two former RMAS tugs. The **Christine** is an example of a class of nine tugs known as the "improved girl class" delivered during the 1960s to the Ministry of Defence for operation by the Port Auxiliary Service. She was built at the yard of Isaac Pimblott & Sons in Northwich and after delivery was based at Devonport. Power comes from a 6-cylinder Lister-Blackstone engine of 659bhp. She left military service in 1990 and was sold to Sea Structures in Plymouth. This company was reported to be in financial difficulties in early 2004 and the tug was sold to Bilberry Shipping in Waterford. Two years later she returned to British ownership when bought by Medway-based Alan &

Annette Pratt. Her modest 6 tonne bollard pull is fine for handling small vessels in the Thames and Medway area and for other contract work which sometimes sees her trading to the near-continent. Without doubt her highest profile task was to tow the supposedly-reconstructed (but actually virtually replicated) **Medway Queen** from Bristol to Gillingham in October 2013. We see the **Christine** in the City Docks in Bristol as she prepares to tow the **Medway Queen** out of Albion Drydock, originally part of the Charles Hill shipyard, on 24 October 2013.

(BMc)

The **Cumbrae** was launched at the Henry Scarr shipyard in Hessle on 27 July 1961 and delivered to the Port Auxiliary Service as **Alsatian** three months later. Power comes from two Lister-Blackstone 8-cylinder engines, each of 659bhp and driving two fixed pitch propellers. Leaving military use in late 1993, she was renamed **Clutha** the following year and fitted with a towing winch. She became **Cumbrae** in 1997. In 2010 she was reported sold to Nigerian buyers and left the River Tyne for Harlingen where she remained. By late 2012 she had been renamed **Juliette Pride II** and had reached Newlyn. There she was detained because of safety issues but she and a sister tug escaped during the night in early March 2013 to make their way to Lagos. This photograph

was taken from the **Anglian Monarch** which had been tasked to assist the **Cumbrae**, in trouble with the barge **Osprey Warrior** off Ramsgate. **Cumbrae**'s towline had parted and whilst picking up the barge's emergency towline in the usual way, fouled one of its rudders and immobilised the tug and tow. **Anglian Monarch** took the barge in tow and was then contracted under a commercial Lloyd's Open Form to take the tug and barge in tow to Dover harbour. Without assistance the barge was in danger of being driven ashore in Force 7 winds. **Cumbrae** and **Osprey Warrior** were in the process of delivering a new and very large crawler crane from Portsmouth to Newcastle.

(DMc)

The **Exact** was built at the Detlef Hegemann Rolandwerft shipyard in Bremen. She was launched in January 1983 and delivered as **Grohn** on 29 September to Unterweser Reederei AG, better known as URAG, at Bremen (see page 79). She is driven by two 6-cylinder Deutz engines, each of 1086bhp, and geared to two directional propellers. This gives her a bollard pull of 25 tonnes. In 1999 she was chartered to Hamburg-based Lütgens & Reimers and was renamed **Exact**. We see her as such at Hamburg in late May 2001. She reverted to her original name when returned to URAG in 2004. In 2011, however, in what seems to be a rather complex arrangement, Lütgens & Reimers took over ownership with the tug remaining under URAG management.

(BMc)

Until the 1980s, Smit Harbour Towage had a virtual monopoly of harbour towage in the huge port of Rotterdam. That monopoly was broken when the Kooren family, involved for many years in deep-sea towage and harbour construction, acquired some modern tugs on the secondhand market and introduced them for harbour towage in Rotterdam. The *ZP Montali* was one of these tugs. She is powered by two Alpha 7-cylinder engines, each of 1600bhp and geared to two Z-peller propulsion units. This gives her a 52 tonne bollard pull.

Delivered in 1985, she was built by Valley Shipbuilding at Brownsville in Texas like other Kooren purchases at the time. She was launched as *ZP Mayacamas* but soon became *ZP Montali*. In the late 1980s the Kooren company became known as Kotug and expanded into the German ports of Hamburg and Bremerhaven. She was photographed at the latter port on 9 August 2007. She left the Kotug ownership and the River Weser in early April 2012 after purchase by the Boluda Group. She was renamed *VB Teckel* and based at Castellon.

(DMc)

The **Flying Osprey** was the third of seven basically similar tugs built at the Mützelfeldtwerft shipyard in Cuxhaven between 1974 and 1982 for Hamburg-based Petersen & Alpers. She was launched on 23 October 1975 and delivered to her owners as **Johanna** on 10 February 1976. Power comes from two Deutz engines, each of 1160bhp and driving two Schottel directional propellers in Kort nozzles. She and sister tug **Karl** were fitted with demountable pushing knees at the stern to facilitate stern-first operation when pushing large barges. Somewhat surprisingly she was sold only six months later and was renamed **Cornelie Wessels** for owners in Emden. In late May 1986 she was acquired by the Alexandra Towing Co Ltd and was renamed **Flying Osprey**. She operated mainly in Southampton and the Solent. She was photographed in Adsteam colours at Southampton on 5 April 2003. In 2005 she was sold to Norwegian owners and was renamed **Boa Sund**. Her main engines were upgraded to 1175bhp and this gave her a bollard pull of 38 tonnes compared to the original 30 tonnes.

(BMc)

The *Arion* is a sistership of the *Johanna* on the previous page and is a long-serving member of the IJmuiden-based Iskes fleet, of which we shall read more. She was the fourth of the seven similar tugs built at the Mützelfeldtwerft yard between 1974 and 1982 for Petersen & Alpers. She was launched on 21 April 1976 and delivered to her owners as *Karl* on 10 June. She and sister vessel *Johanna* differed from the other five in having 8-cylinder Deutz engines each of 1160bhp compared to the 6-cylinder engines each of 870bhp installed in the others. In early November 1985 she was acquired by the Alexandra Towing Co Ltd and was renamed *Flying Kestrel*, working mainly in Southampton along with the *Flying Osprey*. She joined the Iskes fleet as *Arion* in 2000. She has since been fully refurbished and re-engined with two Anglo Belgian Corporation engines each of 1800bhp which give her a bollard pull of 45 tonnes. We see her at IJmuiden in June 2006.

(BMc)

In the mid-1990s, a fleet of tugs was rapidly built up in South Wales under the management of West Coast Towing (UK) Ltd. This company won the contract to handle bulk carriers visiting Port Talbot and soon challenged local operators Alexandra in Swansea and Cory in Newport. The company also entered the market for coastal towage. For conventional shiphandling the company bought several relatively new tugs built in Russia. One of these was the **Alice K**, built at the Gorokhovets shipyard and completed in May 1994. Some sources suggest that she was initially named **Project 269**. The deal to acquire her and a sister tug was complex and rather unconventional. A condition of sale was that the two tugs could not be handed over in Russian waters and so both vessels were handed over to West Coast Towing's **King Loua** in Finnish waters outside Vyborg. The three vessels arrived in South Wales on 5 August 1995. She is driven by two 8-cylinder Pervomaysk engines each of 799bhp and geared to two fixed pitch propellers. This gives her a bollard pull of 25 tonnes. In early 2005 she returned to Russia following purchase by an operator in Kandalaksha and was renamed **Gandvik**. We see her approaching Sharpness on 16 March 2003 prior to drydocking. She retains much of the Wijsmuller livery although her funnel carries the Maltese cross of Svitzer. Wijsmuller had taken over West Coast Towing in 2001.

(BMc)

The **Pasvik**, photographed in Lyme Bay on 4 February 2007 when supporting salvage work on the **MSC Napoli**, is quite different from any other vessel in this book. Officially classed as a tug/supply/pipe carrier, she was built by Stocznia Szczecinska im. A. Warskiego and delivered as **Neftegaz-69** to a Russian company based in Murmansk on 7 September 1990. She was renamed **Pasvik** in 1992. Her two 6-cylinder Sulzer engines provide a total power of 7206bhp and are geared to two controllable pitch propellers, giving her a bollard pull of 80 tonnes. She is also an anchor handler and has a 12.5 ton crane.

Between 2003 and 2007 she was managed by Workships Contractors BV, a Dutch company. In late November 2010 she was one of six tugs used to tow a huge ice-resistant oil production platform, 140 metres wide, from Severodvinsk to Murmansk. At the time of her construction, the communist era in Russia was nearing its end but she possessed certain features which betrayed that communist origin. One of these was a top secret communications room. Even when this photograph was taken, special permission to enter this room had to be obtained.

(DMc)

One of three sister tugs, the **Glengarth** was launched on 10 November 1969 at the Hessle yard of Richard Dunston Ltd and was delivered on 27 February 1970 to R & J H Rea Ltd and registered in Milford Haven. Later that year, ownership was transferred to Cory Ship Towage Ltd. She was powered by a single 9-cylinder Ruston engine of 2460bhp manufactured by English Electric Diesels Ltd and driving a single fixed-pitch propeller within a steerable Kort nozzle. This arrangement gave her a bollard pull of 35 tonnes. The tug was sold in 1996 to Shannon Tugs Ltd, which had been incorporated as an associate company of Cory Towage in 1991 with Cory having a 50% holding. After five years under the Irish flag, she was bought by owners in Setubal and in 2003 was renamed **Barra de Setubal**. In 2009 she suffered a serious main engine breakdown and was sold to a Dutch broker for onward sale. On 11 December 2009 she arrived at Stellendam in the Netherlands and four days later moved to a shipyard at Maaskant. In mid-July 2012 she was reported to have been sold to shipbreakers at Ghent. We see her in Milford Haven in May 1987.

(BMc)

The construction of two new terminals on Milford Haven to handle the import of liquefied natural gas in the early years of this century required a new generation of tugs. The contract to supply these was awarded to Svitzer which already operated the Haven tug fleet. Nine new tugs were built in total and five of these, including the **Svitzer Haven**, were of a class termed RAstar 3400 from the Vancouver-based naval architects Robert Allan Ltd. Three of the five, again including **Svitzer Haven**, are powered by two 16-cylinder GE Marine main engines, each of 3912bhp and geared to Schottel fully steerable propulsion units incorporating controllable pitch propellers. This arrangement provides a bollard pull of 107 tonnes, well over the 95 tonnes specified in the building contract. Like her sister vessels, the **Svitzer Haven** was built by Construcciones Navales Paulino Freire from whose shipyard in Vigo she was delivered on 20 March 2009. A feature of the design is a significant outward flare on the upper sides of the hull. When the tug heels over, a large righting force is generated and thus improves stability as well as increasing towline force. Our photograph shows her escorting an inward bound gas tanker on 11 June 2009.

(DMc)

47

It had been the custom of many traditional tug operators in the UK to give local names to their tugs. When Svitzer came to dominate UK towage during the first decade of the new millennium, this company tried to follow the custom but it was never going to be successful because of frequent changes of operational base for the tugs. An early attempt saw the delivery of sister tugs **Svitzer Bristol** and **Svitzer Brunel** to the Bristol area after construction by Astilleros Zamakona at Santurtzi near Bilbao. Illustrating the futility of local names, the **Svitzer Brunel** was transferred to the River Thames in November 2011. She was launched as **Severngarth** on 15 June 2003 and delivered as **Svitzer Brunel** on 16 September. She has a bollard pull of 58 tonnes and is powered by two 6-cylinder Niigata engines each of 2200bhp driving two Z-peller units. Although based on the English side of the Bristol Channel, we see her proudly displaying the Welsh dragon at Swansea on 15 April 2005.

(Chris Jones)

Economic "liberalisation" within the European Union in the mid-1990s saw Dutch tugs start to appear in Hamburg with a 40% subsidy from the Dutch government for crew wages. Not surprisingly, this started a tug battle in the German port but it was a further six years before the subsidy was deemed illegal. In the meantime, the Hamburg-based Fairplay company seized the opportunity to establish a towing operation in the Netherlands and ordered four tugs to work in Rotterdam with an option for two more. The first four, **Fairplay 21** –

Fairplay 24, were built at Vigo but the builders suffered financial problems and delivery was delayed. The two further vessels were built at a different yard. Like her three sisters, the **Fairplay 23** is fitted with two 8-cylinder Deutz engines each of 2238bhp. These drive two fixed pitch directional propellers in Kort nozzles, providing a bollard pull of 52 tonnes. The photograph was taken during the annual World Harbour Days celebration in Rotterdam on 3 September 2011.

(BMc)

The Dutch company Heerema began as a small construction company based near Lake Maracaibo in Venezuela. Expertise gained in that area proved to be of huge significance during the development of oil fields in the North Sea in the 1960s and 1970s. In 1982, Heerema took delivery of two anchor handling tugs from the Niestern Sander Shipyard in Delfzijl. The second of these was the *Retriever*. A powerful tug, she is driven by two 16-cylinder MaK engines each of 5996bhp which drive two controllable pitch propellers. She has a bollard pull of 160 tonnes. She was replaced by a newer vessel in 2013 and in May 2014 was sold to Nigerian owners. She was renamed *Roma* under the flag of St Vincent and the Grenadines but was laid up in Rotterdam in August 2014. We see her at Rotterdam in May 2006 as she assists the *Thialf*, a few details of which are on the next page.

(DMc)

Details of the **Smit Humber** are very similar to those of the **Smit Loire** (page 58). Certainly her construction and technical details are identical. The main difference between the two is that the **Smit Humber** has no firefighting equipment. She was delivered to Smit on 28 April 2000. She has passed through the ownership of several Smit subsidiary companies and was registered in the Bahamas during spring 2009. In mid-2010, she was working at Freeport, Bahamas. She transferred to Canadian registry in summer 2011 and after working initially at Vancouver she then moved north to Prince Rupert and has continued to work between those two ports since that time. We see her, and the **Retriever** on the previous page, moving the huge Heerema-owned crane barge **Thialf** in the Caland Canal near Rotterdam in May 2006. The **Thialf** is technically termed a deepwater construction vessel and its two cranes are capable of a tandem lift of 14,200 tonnes.

(DMc)

In 1971, Alexandra placed an order for four tugs with the Richard Dunston shipyard in Hessle. Launched on 20 December 1971 and delivered the following March, the **Crosby** was the second of the four. The first three, **Albert**, **Crosby** and **Alfred**, were for work on the Mersey whilst the fourth, **Victoria**, was initially placed at Swansea but later saw work at Southampton and Felixstowe. All four were also used to tow huge production platforms from construction sites in Scotland. They were very popular tugs with owner, crews and pilots. She is driven by a 9-cylinder Ruston engine geared to a fixed pitch propeller and providing a bollard pull of 40 tonnes. After the arrival in the Mersey of the **Canada** (page 18) and **Collingwood**, it was intended to transfer the group of three. The **Albert** joined **Victoria** (very appropriately!) on the Solent and **Alfred** moved to Felixstowe. The plan to transfer the **Crosby** there was aborted. She was sold to owners in Setubal in 1999 and renamed **Montebelo**. Later switching to the Spanish flag and being painted all over in orange, she was seen at Burriana and Mahon, but was noted at Motril in poor external condition in spring 2014. This view, taken on 18 August 1981, enables the reader to see what a Kort nozzle looks like.

(BMc)

While being towed to new owners in Greece on 18 October 1981 three former Mersey-based Alexandra tugs came adrift and ended up on the rocks at Solva, Pembrokeshire. The **Vernicos Giorgis** was towing the other two. She was built as **Pea Cock** by Cammell Laird at Birkenhead and was launched on 30 November 1959 with completion coming in January 1960. Power came from a 6-cylinder Ruston engine of 1200bhp. Her owners were North West Tugs Ltd, managed by the pioneering Liverpool Screw Towing Company which had been responsible for the first screw tugs on the Mersey and the first motor tugs designed specially for service on that river. In December 1966, the latter company and its subsidiary came into the ownership of Alexandra but it was not until 1970 that the tugs were renamed with the **Pea Cock** becoming **Canada**. Ten years later she was renamed **Canada II** to release the name for a newbuilding (see page 18). In the following year she was sold to Nicolas E Vernicos, of Piraeus, and renamed **Vernicos Genevieve**. For some reason, there was a change of mind and she became **Vernicos Giorgis** (also noted as **Vernicos Giorgios**) while still in drydock in Birkenhead. This rare photograph, taken on 18 August 1981, shows the name change taking place.

(BMc)

The **MSC Viking** was the third of four identical tugs delivered to the Manchester Ship Canal Company in the mid-1970s from the Wivenhoe shipyard of James W Cook & Co Ltd. Towage on the Canal remained the responsibility of the Canal Company until 1989 when ownership of the four V-class tugs was handed over to the family-owned Carmet Tug Company Ltd. Nowadays two tugs are always available at very short notice and one is on standby. The tugs are kept in immaculate condition with each having a unique identifying feature. As far as the **MSC Viking** is concerned, that feature is the top of her wheelhouse which is now painted blue. Power comes from two Allen engines, each of 640bhp and geared to two fixed pitch propellers and giving a bollard pull of 16 tonnes. Our photograph was taken on the outskirts of Warrington on 26 August 1979 when she was still owned by the Manchester Ship Canal Company.

(BMc)

The **Goliath**, seen at Barry in June 1989, was built by P K Harris at Appledore as **MSC Scimitar** for the Manchester Ship Canal Company. She was launched on 6 September 1956 and delivered on 19 November. She has two 6-cylinder Ruston & Hornsby engines totalling 1290bhp geared to two fixed pitch propellers. She was sold to Spithead Trading Limited in 1987 and was eventually renamed **Goliath**. In the ensuing years she had various modifications which made her suitable for a wide variety of tasks especially involving seagoing and coastal work which would be very different from shiphandling in the confined waters of the Manchester Ship Canal. Following her sale, navigational and communications equipment had to be immediately upgraded. She was fitted with anchors, windlass, and a twin-drum towing and anchor-handling winch on the after deck. Additions also included a powerful bow thruster and firefighting monitors. In 1991, she was equipped with a "Clip-On". This was a demountable accommodation unit adapted from the upper section of former sister vessel **MSC Sceptre**. Since 1997 she has been operated by Griffin Towage & Marine.

(BMc)

In late 1953, Tees Towing took delivery of the **Caedmon Cross**, the first tug for a British owner to have direct geared diesel drive. So pleased was the company with this tug after six months in service that two more were ordered from the same builder, namely Scott & Sons at Bowling. The second of the pair was the **Ingleby Cross**, delivered in October 1955. All three had a 4-cylinder Crossley engine of 750bhp providing a bollard pull of 9 tonnes. She was acquired by Fowey Harbour Commissioners in 1968 and was renamed **Gribbin Head**. Two decades later she was bought by Haven Towing Co Ltd after suffering engine damage and she was fitted with a new English Electric engine of 1250bhp. In 1990 her owners were taken over by West Coast Towing and she sported this company's colours only briefly as she was sold later in the year to Tuskar Rock Diving Co Ltd and renamed **Tuskar Rock**. It was in 2006 that she was reported to have been sold to Spanish operators in Huelva and she was noted at Valletta in 2007. Four years later, she was understood to have been renamed **Triva II**. We see her laid up at Pembroke Dock in August 1988.

(BMc)

The **St Denys** was built in 1919 at the William Beardmore shipyard at Dalmuir on the River Clyde. Power came from a 3-cylinder steam engine with Caprotti poppet valve gear, a rare example of a marine engine thus fitted. She was originally named **Northgate Scot** and it was only in 1959 that she was named after a Cornish saint. She was taken out of service by the Falmouth Towage Company in 1982 and was acquired by Falmouth Maritime Museum. The cost of maintaining the tug as a visitor attraction at Custom House Quay, where she was photographed in late March 1985, proved beyond the means of the volunteers who looked after her and in 1991 she was sold to a museum at Douarnenez in Brittany where she remains.

(BMc)

The hull of the **Smit Loire** was built by Stocznia Polnocna (Northern Shipyard) in Gdansk and she was completed at the Damen shipyard in Gorinchem. Power comes from two Wärtsilä 6-cylinder engines, each of 2488bhp and geared to two Aquamaster directional propellers. This arrangement provides a bollard pull of 65 tonnes. We see her at Europoort on 26 January 2005. In spring 2008, the **Smit Loire** was hired by the Port Qasim Authority for a period of two years to give assistance to the larger ships visiting the port. This charter, or more exactly the tendering process leading to it, proved to be a matter of considerable controversy within Pakistan. She was noted at Cape Town in early May 2008 taking on bunkers and supplies. Since mid-2013, the **Smit Loire** has been working at Freeport in the Bahamas.

(DMc)

The **Smit Rusland** was launched at the De Merwede shipyard in Hardinxveld on 11 May 1979 and delivered to Smit Vos B.V. on 28 June. She is driven by two Kromhout 6-cylinder engines with a total power output of 1900bhp. The engines are reverse reduction geared to two Promac controllable pitch propellers and provide a bollard pull of 28 tonnes. She is seen on the New Waterway on 27 October 2003. In summer 2012 she was sold, along with sistership **Smit Zweden**, to a company based in Gibraltar. On 8 August 2012, she was renamed **Rusland** and transferred to the flag of St Vincent & the Grenadines.

Two days later the tugs left Rotterdam with a destination given variously as Tangier or Ksar es-Seghir. In fact, they were heading for the new port of Tanger-Med, some 40 kilometres east of Tangier. The tugs were to be used for towing construction and dredging equipment along the coasts of North and West Africa. The change of owner, flag and name were only ever going to be temporary and soon after arrival the **Rusland** was renamed **Ureca XIII** under the flag of Papua New Guinea, changing to Equatorial Guinea in 2013 and in the ownership of SOMAGEC, a huge African construction company.

(DMc)

Bugsier Reederei Und Bergungs AG was a comparative newcomer to the ship towage scene in Hamburg, arriving in 1954 and challenging the status quo with four new tugs built by F Schichau in Bremerhaven. A decade later the Bugsier company returned to the yard for a further four tugs, the second of these being **Bugsier 29** which was launched on 14 December 1964 and delivered on 1 February 1965. All four were fitted with a 6-cylinder Deutz engine of 800 bhp driving a fixed pitch propeller in a Kort nozzle and giving a bollard pull of 14 tonnes. In 1993 she was sold to operators in Northern Ireland and renamed **Mourne Shore** for work in Carlingford Lough where she was photographed on 9 December 2006. She is always in immaculate condition and can be seen at the ports of Greenore and Warrenpoint.

(DMc)

Seen at Falmouth in May 1986, the **Wotan** was one of four large salvage tugs built for Bugsier between 1972 and 1975. She was a product of the F Schichau shipyard in Bremerhaven and was delivered to Bugsier on 22 August 1972. Power came from two 12-cylinder Deutz diesel engines, each of 4400bhp, and she had a 125 tonne bollard pull. During a refit in 1979 two fixed Kort nozzles were added and this improved her bollard pull to 135 tonnes. In 1986, the directors of Bugsier decided to transfer some of its tugs to the Cypriot flag but the consequent replacement of dedicated German crews with inexperienced foreign crews proved unsuccessful. The **Wotan** hoisted the Cypriot flag at Galveston on 12 November 1987. On 6 July 1990, she met heavy weather off the Dutch coast when towing a floating dock from Bremerhaven to Algiers. When attempting to reconnect after a wire had parted, she was rammed by the dock and sank. She was raised on 30 August and towed to Eemshaven. Declared a total loss, she arrived at Bremerhaven two weeks later for the removal of usable parts and engines. Subsequently she arrived at Zeebrugge for demolition on 26 November 1990.

(BMc)

Powered by two 6-cylinder Ruston engines with a total output of 3514hp and geared to two Aquamaster propulsion units, the **Deben** was built for the Alexandra Towing Co Ltd by Richards (Shipbuilders) at Great Yarmouth and launched on 20 November 1989. She was intended to work in the Felixstowe fleet. Following the Howard Smith and Adsteam takeovers, she was renamed **Adsteam Deben** in 2005. Genuine competition among the towage companies on the Humber has remained strong and in August 2006, Adsteam decided to increase the competition by introducing its own cut-rate operation to which it gave the name Humber Tugs Ltd. Eventually a fleet of five tugs was established, all transferred from other areas and the **Adsteam Deben** became **HT Blade** in the Humber Tugs fleet. However also in 2006 negotiations started for Svitzer to take over Adsteam and this was completed in 2007. In 2011 the **HT Blade** was sold to Russian operators and, now renamed **STS Star**, left the River Tees on 28 May 2011 supposedly heading for service at Kerch but in 2014 she was working at the Russian port of Novorossiysk. We see her in Howard Smith livery at Felixstowe on 1 April 1995.

(Ian Willett)

The **Lady Madeleine** is an example of the Damen 3211 design – a development of that builder's earlier 3110. The development started in 1994 when an increase in required bollard pull was envisaged by sales and product management teams of Damen Shipyards. The tug's hull was built at Gdansk with completion at the Damen shipyard in Gorinchem. Power comes from two 6-cylinder Ruston engines each of 2447bhp. They are geared to two Aquamaster units under the stern and are able to give the tug a bollard pull of 61 tonnes ahead. She was part of a newbuilding programme valued at £18 million and was delivered to Howard Smith Towage in July 1996 to operate from Sheerness on the River Medway while her two sisters, **Bentley** and **Melton**, were delivered to the Howard Smith operation in Felixstowe. Adsteam took over Howard Smith in May 2001 and the **Lady Madeleine** was transferred to Southampton. In 2007 Adsteam was taken over by Svitzer and the tug was renamed **Svitzer Madeleine** the following year. By 2013 she was based on the Humber. Here we see her after assisting a container ship into Southampton Container Terminal on 2 June 2007.

(BMc)

The **Herculaneum** was launched at the Northwich yard of W J Yarwood & Sons Ltd on 30 August 1962 and was delivered to the Alexandra Towing Company Ltd in December of that year. She was an experimental tug with power coming from an 8-cylinder Alpha engine of 960bhp geared to a controllable pitch propeller within a steerable Kort nozzle. It was the first time that this combination had been used in the Alexandra fleet and it gave her a 15 tonne bollard pull. A notable piece of equipment was a patent slip towing hook designed by Alexandra's superintendent engineer. After a decade working on the Mersey, she moved to Swansea in 1972. We see her at that port as she assists the tanker **British Beech** on 16 August 1986. Her first change of name came in 1997 when she was sold to Honduran-flag operators by whom she was renamed **Atlas**. Three years later, she became **Christos VIII** under the Greek flag. Some reports suggest that she was subsequently re-engined with a Cummins engine of 1000bhp but *Lloyd's Register* makes no reference to such a change. In mid-2014 she was based on the island of Mykonos.

(BMc)

Having been in the fleets of three competing towage companies, the **Hurricane H** can certainly establish a claim to fame. As **Margam**, she was the second of a pair of tugs ordered by the Alexandra Towing Company Ltd to handle the largest bulk carriers visiting the new tidal harbour at Port Talbot which served the huge adjacent steel works. Both tugs were built at the Hessle shipyard of Richard Dunston Ltd and were given local Welsh names. The **Mumbles** was delivered in February 1969 and the **Margam** followed in November 1970 having been launched on 17 August. Power comes from a 9-cylinder Ruston engine of 2190bhp geared to a fixed pitch propeller, giving a bollard pull of 40 tonnes. She was notable in being the only tug in Britain fitted with a two-speed gearbox to enable optimum engine revolutions for towing or for free running. She was hugely popular with her crews and was occasionally called up to Scotland for work associated with the construction of oil rigs. It came as a shock when West Coast Towing Ltd, a fledgling towage company set up to compete with Howard Smith and Cory in South Wales, won the contract to provide towage services at Port Talbot from early February 1997. Even more of a shock was the sale of the **Margam** to the new company by whom she was renamed **Hurricane H**. She remained under this name when Wijsmuller took over West Coast Towing in early May 2001. We see her off Swansea on 6 September 2005. Abortive sales were reported in 2007 and early 2008 and she is understood to have been renamed **Hurricane** briefly in early 2008. In mid-2008, however, the tug was bought by Poseidon Salvage International, a Piraeus-based company established in 1992. She was renamed **Voukefalas** under the Panamanian flag. In mid-2014 she was working at Tema in Ghana.

(DMc)

We now return to tugs built for service on the River Thames. The order for the *Canada* (see page 18) was won by the McTay yard against competition form other yards which had traditionally built tugs for Alexandra. Clearly the company was impressed by the *Canada* for it placed orders for five further tugs from the McTay yard between 1982 and 1990. The first of these was the *Sun Thames*, designed to work in the Alexandra fleet on the river from which she took her name. Launched on 10 March 1982 and delivered the following month, she was moved to Ramsgate in spring 1986 but later returned to the Thames and we see her off Tilbury on 28 September 2004. She went through the Howard Smith and Adsteam eras until 2006 when she became part of the Humber Tugs fleet as *HT Sword*. Renamed *Svitzer Sword* in 2009 while working on the River Tyne, this name was short-lived as she was sold to owners in Constanta, Romania, becoming *BSV Anglia* in 2010. Power comes from two 6-cylinder Ruston engines each of 1339bhp and geared to two Voith-Schneider propellers. She has a bollard pull of 31 tonnes.

(Ian Willett)

The first of two sister vessels, the **Sun Surrey** was launched at the Great Yarmouth shipyard of Richards Shipbuilders Ltd on 11 November 1991 and delivered to the Alexandra Towing Co Ltd on 20 March of the following year. She is driven by two 6-cylinder Ruston engines with a total output of 3826bhp and geared to two forward-mounted Voith-Schneider propulsion units. She has a bollard pull of 43 tonnes. She and sister tug **Sun Sussex** were built with extra accommodation as it was intended that they would serve the oil refineries on the Thames which would require tugs to be fully manned at all times. In 2004 she moved to the Solent and we see her in Adsteam livery at Southampton on 3 September 2004. She was later renamed **Adsteam Surrey** and became **Svitzer Surrey** in October 2009.

(BMc)

The company now known as Iskes Towage and Salvage started in 1928 and was acquired by Ben Iskes in 1968. Initially the company tugs served only IJmuiden where the fishing fleet had grown rapidly earlier in the 1960s but it later started to assist vessels along the North Sea Canal to and from Amsterdam. The company has expanded rapidly during the new millennium, acquiring newbuildings whilst still retaining several older vessels. The *Pollux* was built at the Schichau shipyard in Bremerhaven in 1963 for Hapag Lloyd and entered the Iskes fleet in 1993 without change of name. In the previous year, Iskes had signed its first written contract. This was with Cool Carriers who required a tug with a bollard pull of 20 tonnes to handle their refrigerated vessels. The *Pollux* was ideal but required modifications. In 1993 she was fitted with a new wheelhouse and her two Deutz engines, geared to two Voith-Schneider propellers, were upgraded to 1600bhp and gave her a 20 tonne bollard pull. She went on to have an important place in the company's history as she undertook its first coastal towage duty by towing a floating crane from IJmuiden to the Hook of Holland in November 1993.

(DMc)

Early in 2001, Iskes Towage & Salvage announced an order for its first newbuilding. The **Thetis** was to be a Delta Azimuth Tug 2800 vessel from the IHC Delta Shipyard at Sliedrecht, the first ASD shiphandling tug to be completed by the yard. The hull was built at Bezdanin Croatia and launched on 11 February 2002 but the tug was not completed for well over a year, delivery to her owners being made on 11 June 2003.

Power comes from two 9-cylinder Wartsila engines, each of 2298bhp and geared to two Z-peller propulsion units. This gives her a bollard pull of 61 tonnes. In recent years, she has carried the slogan "Chartered and operated by Svitzer". We see her emerging from the locks at her home port of IJmuiden in late May 2006.

(DMc)

Built by Matsuura Tekko Zosen at Hiroshima, Japan, and delivered on 8 February 1999 to Klyne Tugs to work in the North Sea, the *Anglian Monarch* was however contracted to the Maritime and Coastguard Agency for the winters of 1999 and 2000 to stand-by as an Emergency Towing Vessel (ETV) in the Minches/Fair Isle area. From 2001 when Klyne Tugs were awarded the contract to provide full ETV coverage at four locations around the UK coast, the *Anglian Monarch* was almost exclusively stationed in the Dover Straits, partly due to her poor sea-keeping abilities compared to other vessels in the fleet but also because this station requires the tug to spend more time steaming and

the *Anglian Monarch* was one of the more economical tugs in the fleet. Anchoring in the Dover Straits can be quite difficult, with strong winds and tides combining to make the likelihood of dragging quite a possibility and it was for this reason the *Anglian Monarch* was seen alongside in the French port of Boulogne on 29 December 2006. She was chartered jointly by the British and French authorities to provide emergency towage and counter pollution services in the Dover Straits so her time was therefore split equally on the French and English sides of the Channel. Sold in 2013, she was renamed *Resolve Monarch*.

(DMc)

The **Anglian Sovereign** was delivered in 2003 to Klyne Tugs (Lowestoft) Ltd for use as an ETV on charter to the UK's Maritime and Coastguard Agency, and was sister of the **Anglian Princess** delivered in 2002. Both were built at Yantai Raffles yard in China. She Is a Rolls-Royce Ulstein UT719-T design fitted with two Wärtsilä engines each of 8,250bhp and driving two controllable pitch propellers in fixed nozzles. The tugs are also fitted with two 800hp bow thrusters and one 900hp stern thruster. The bollard pull is 180 tonnes. The photograph was taken at Scalloway on a very still but bitterly cold 25 December 2004.

The **Anglian Sovereign** was usually the Fair Isle ETV with crew changes and stores regularly being done at Scalloway, and less often Kirkwall. The tug often spent the summer months doing survey work around the Shetland and Orkney islands after specialist equipment was fitted during 2005 to facilitate this. Klyne Tugs was sold to Rochester-based J P Knight in December 2007 and the MCA contract ended in 2011. The **Anglian Sovereign** was sold to Smit Transport Belgium and then to Unie van Redding en Sleepdienst (URS), both parts of the Boskalis group, and has been renamed **Union Sovereign**.

(DMc)

In the mid-1970s, the River Tees began to handle much larger ships than hitherto. This was because of the opening of Redcar Ore Terminal and also the later start of crude oil exports from the Ekofisk Field in the North Sea. New tugs were needed and the *Yarm Cross* was the fourth of a radical and distinctive new design, although the tugs were not identical sisterships. Built at the Richard Dunston shipyard in Hessle, she was launched on 24 May 1979 and delivered to Tees Towing Co Ltd on 29 August. Ownership was transferred to Cory Towage (Tees) Ltd in 1990 and the next twelve years saw various changes of ownership as a result of takeovers and mergers. She is powered by two 6-cylinder Ruston engines giving a total of 2640bhp and providing a bollard pull of 35.5 tonnes. We see her on the River Tyne as she assists the vehicle carrier *Pacific Spirit* on 6 March 2006. In 2012, she was sold to Black Sea Services in Constanta, Romania, and was renamed *BSV Scotia*. She left Swansea on 10 November along with *Yewgarth*, towed by *Pantodynamos*.

(DMc)

The **Stackgarth** was another of the group of tugs built at the Hessle shipyard of Richard Dunston in the late 1980s and early 1990s for the Tees Towing Company. Launched as **Eston Cross** on 20 February 1985, she was completed on 29 March of the following year. Power comes from two 6-cylinder Ruston engines totalling 3400bhp and geared to twin Aquamaster multidirectional propellers mounted forward. She has a bollard pull of 43 tonnes. In August 1990, Tees Towing was taken over by Cory Towage but the **Eston Cross** was not renamed until she transferred to Milford Haven in 1994 and assumed the local name of **Stackgarth**. The late 1990s saw her working at Liverpool and Belfast before moving to Swansea in October 1998. In summer 1999, her superstructure was modified to improve visibility. She soon became part of the Bristol-based fleet. We see her as she leaves Avonmouth dock and enters the Bristol Channel on a June evening in 2004. She later moved to the River Tyne and in 2010 was sold to an operator in Waterford by whom she was renamed **Fastnet Nore**.

(DMc)

We now take a brief look at some tugs in northern Europe. During the twentieth century one of the busiest yards for tug construction in Scandinavia was AB Åsiverken at Åmål on Lake Vänern in Sweden. In 1979 this yard built the **Veronica** for Luleå Bogserbåts AB, a company established in 1971 and owned by the municipality of Luleå in northern Sweden which sought to keep its port open throughout the year and required tugs to do so. Although originally named **Veronica** she became **Victoria** in 1981 when that name became available following

the sale of the previous **Victoria** which had been the first tug owned by Luleå Bogserbåts AB. In 1980 she was chartered to CL Hanssons Bogserings AB in Gothenburg but returned the next year. Power comes from a 16-cylinder Nohab Polar engine of 2640bhp geared to a controllable pitch propeller and providing a bollard pull of 25 tonnes. In addition to shiphandling locally, the three tugs in the fleet are required for icebreaking at other ports in northern Sweden during winter months.

(BMc)

Between 1910 and 1915, Johannes Håkans bought two small tugs to assist in transporting timber to his sawmill In Finland. In the 1920s, his son Alfons joined the business and gave his name to a company which would own one of the largest tug fleets in Scandinavia. Income from successful salvage operations and the ever-expanding timber trade enable the company to take over others and build up its fleet. The

Neptun was built at the Hollming shipyard in Rauma where she was launched on 19 February 1980. She was delivered as *Heimo Saarinen* on 15 April to O/Y Hangon Hinaus, a company purchased by Håkans in 1988, and was renamed *Neptun* in the following year. Power comes from a 9-cylinder Wärtsilä engine of 3910bhp geared to a fixed pitch propeller. She was photographed at Rauma on 30 June 2007.

(BMc)

The **Haabull** was launched at the Aalesund shipyard of A M Liaaen on 20 October 1978 and delivered to Stavanger-based owners A/S Haaland & Sonn in December of that year. Her two Klöckner-Humboldt-Deutz engines, each of 1249bhp, are geared to two directional propellers and provide a bollard pull of 35 tonnes. In 2000 her owner was listed as Oslo-based Neptun Rederi but within two years she had entered the fleet of Buksér og Berging, the largest tug operator in Norway and also based in Oslo. We see her passing through the Karmsund in Norway on 25 May 2006. In September 2007 she was bought by Otto Wulf, based in Cuxhaven, and was renamed **Taucher O Wulf 4** under the German flag.

(BMc)

WUZ Port & Marine Service Co Ltd was established in the port of Gdansk soon after the port was privatised in 1991. The company's tugs, in their distinctive orange livery, have become a feature of the port since that time. The **Ares** was built in Gdynia by Stocznia Marynarki Wojennej im Dabrowszczakow in 1976. She is powered by a 12-cylinder Fiat engine of 2500hp driving a controllable pitch propeller and this gives her a bollard pull of 31 tonnes. She was photographed at Gdansk on 6 August 2003.

(BMc)

The **Hermes** was built at D W Kremer Sohn shipyard in Elmshorn and launched in March 1978. On 28 March of that year, her builders were declared bankrupt and so she and sister vessel **Bremen** were towed to Husum on 30 April for completion by Husumer Schiffswerft. On 26 July she was delivered as **Bremerhaven** to URAG - Unterweser Reederei AG at Bremen and was sold to the Aarhus Port Authority in Denmark on 25 July 1986. Her 8-cylinder MaK engine of 3000bhp drives a single fixed pitch propeller in a steerable Kort nozzle. She has a bollard pull of 46 tonnes. We see her at Aarhus in May 2005.

(BMc)

After a former member of the URAG fleet, we move to a current one. Photographed at the tug base in Bremen on 25 August 2014, the **Berne** is the third tug to have carried this name. Built locally at the Detlef Hegemann Rolandwerft shipyard in Bremen and launched on 12 July 1985, she was delivered to URAG on 27 September and is one of four basically similar tugs built at the yard for URAG during the mid-1980s. URAG was founded by merchants from Bremen under the name "Schleppschiffahrtsgesellschaft Unterweser" (SGUW) in 1890 and in 1922 became Unterweser Reederei Aktiengesellschaft with its usual abbreviation of URAG. The **Berne** is driven by two 6-cylinder Deutz engines, each of 1088bhp and connected to a Voith-Schneider propeller, this arrangement giving her a bollard pull of 25.5 tonnes.

(BMc)

The **Champagne** was built at the Dieppe yard of Ateliers et Chantiers de la Manche in 1979. Delivered on 10 May 1979, she entered service as **Marseillais 18** but by the end of the year she had been renamed **Chambon Mistral**. In 1989, she was chartered by Kotug and her name was modified to **Mistral** under the flag of the Bahamas. Returning to French operation in 1993, she became **Abeille Champagne**. Following purchase by Italian owners in 2002 she was renamed **Champagne** and then in March 2011 she was renamed **Canal Services 15** after being bought by owners in Romania. Her two 12-cylinder MWM engines drive two Voith-Schneider propellers and provide a bollard pull of 45 tonnes. She was photographed in the Adriatic Sea in November 2009.

(DMc)

Remolcadores de Barcelona was founded in 1886 and since that time has provided towage services in the port of Barcelona. Now part of Grupo Rebarsa, it has expanded to other ports on the Catalan Mediterranean coast. The **Montornes**, photographed at Barcelona in August 1997, was built in 1992 by Astilleros Zamakona at Santurce, Bilbao. In 2004 the tug was sold to Bambini Srl, Ravenna, and was renamed **Mario B** under the Italian flag. This company specialises in crew boats and workboats and the **Mario B** became the most powerful tug in its small fleet of such vessels. She is driven by a single 9-cylinder Nomo engine of 2750bhp geared to a fixed pitch propeller. This gives her a bollard pull of 43 tonnes.

(BMc)

The **Portgarth**, seen in drydock at Sharpness in July 1975, was one of a pair of tugs ordered by J Cooper (Belfast) Ltd from the Gateshead yard of T Mitchison Ltd. She was launched as **Cashel** on 7 November 1958 with sister tug **Clonmel** being launched on 22 January 1959. These two tugs, intended for service at the Whitegate oil refinery, are understood to be the only ones built with a hydroconic hull design at the Mitchison yard. Power came from a 6-cylinder Polar engine geared to a controllable pitch propeller and giving her a bollard pull of 22 tonnes. She entered the Cory fleet in 1970 and on 15 February 1973 left Cobh for Avonmouth, being re-registered in Bristol. She was renamed **Portgarth** in the following year. In early 1981 she was sold to Piraeus-based Nicolas E Vernicos and left the Bristol Channel on 7 April 1981 on passage to the Mersey where, now named **Vernicos Martha**, she collected two other tugs purchased by the Greek owner and towed them to Greece. A transfer within the Vernicos group saw her become **Aghios Nikolaos** in 1989. She was reported to be still working in 2010 but nothing has since been heard of her.

(BMc collection)

Alexandra Towing had always been a good customer of the Cochrane shipyard in Selby. In the early 1950s, three large steam tugs were ordered and these were followed some three years later by three smaller vessels. The first of the latter was the **Waterloo**, launched on 24 October 1953 and delivered in April 1954. She was powered by a 3-cylinder steam engine manufactured by C D Holmes. Despite her Merseyside name, she worked at Swansea until 1962. She was then converted to burn fuel oil and worked on the Mersey before returning to Swansea. We see her in drydock in Cardiff on 14 January 1972. This could possibly have been a sale docking as she left Swansea on 14 February following sale to Rimorchiatori Napoletani in Naples by whom she was renamed renamed **Dritto**. She was scrapped in Naples in 1989.

(John Wiltshire)

The **New Ross 1** was completed by Arklow Marine in 1986. Fitted with a Gardner engine, she was used by the port after which she was named mainly to handle barges filled with silt dredged from the bed of the River Barrow. She saw occasional use in maintaining the navigation lights on the river and she sometimes assisted ships without bow thrusters that called at New Ross. Tragedy struck on 8 August 1995 when she was assisting the tanker *Grizzly* which was arriving at Great Island Power Station about 8 miles down river. The tug was fast aft and was easing the stern of the tanker towards the jetty when a sudden engine movement by the tanker caught the tug beam on and she capsized. Sadly her crew of two both died. The tug was salved and rebuilt with a Caterpillar engine of 550bhp geared to a single screw in a Kort nozzle and giving her a bollard pull of about 7 tonnes. She was acquired by Cardiff Commercial Boat Operators and used to support various civil engineering projects in South Wales. Occasionally she was called across to the River Avon to escort larger vessels using the river and it was there that she was photographed on 5 August 2006.

(BMc)

The **Bristolian** was built at the Gorinchem yard of Damen Marine Services and completed as **Zal 4** in early December 1979. An example of the Damen Pushycat 1500 standard design, she has a 12-cylinder Caterpillar engine of 550bhp which gives her a bollard pull of just over 5 tonnes. In July 1980 she was acquired by Dordrecht-based Rederij T Muller and was renamed **En Avant 9**. In mid-2003 she came into British ownership when bought by H & S Marine Ltd for whom she worked as **Herman Jr**. Bought by Bristol City Council in 2007 and renamed **Bristolian**, she is an ideal vessel for escorting larger vessels using the River Avon in addition to more general duties within the City Docks which, although seeing virtually no commercial shipping, still require constant maintenance. She was photographed in the Cumberland Basin on 17 March 2009.

(BMc)

We stay with smaller multipurpose vessels and look at the **Knab** which was built by Mandal Slip & Mekaniske Vaerft at Mandal in Norway and delivered to the Lerwick Harbour Trust in 1980. The title of her owner changed to Lerwick Port Authority in 1999. She is powered by two Gardner 8-cylinder engines with an output of 460bhp and has a bollard pull of 7 tonnes. At Lerwick, she served as a pilot vessel in addition to her towage duties. Replaced in 2006 by a brand new **Knab**, she was sold to Humber-based Marine Services (Grimsby) Ltd and renamed **Knap**. She has been used for occasional shiphandling at Grimsby and also for marine support work on Humberside. We see her in Bressay Sound in July 1993 strongly backlit as the sun sets beyond Lerwick in the distance.

(BMc)

The **Afon Alaw**, seen arriving at Barry in April 1990, was built in 1975 at the De Hoop shipyard in Hardinxveld-Giessendam. Along with **Afon Braint**, she was designed for work at the single-point tanker mooring buoy at Amlwch off the north coast of Anglesey. She has two 8-cylinder Caterpillar engines, each of 575hp, driving two fixed-pitch propellers. The two vessels were owned by Risdon Beazley Marine Ltd and operated by Buoywork (Anglesey) Ltd, an associate of Holyhead Towing Company. By the late 1980s, the Amlwch terminal was no longer being used and the **Afon Alaw** was taken over by Holyhead Towing and painted in their colours. In 1991 she was sold to Ravenna-based Gestioni Marittime and was renamed **Picchio** under the Italian flag.

(BMc)

The **Sir Bevois**, named after the legendary founder of Southampton, is one of a pair of tugs ordered by the Southampton Isle of Wight and South of England Royal Mail Steam Packet Company Limited, better known as Red Funnel, to work in the Solent and is the third vessel to carry this name. She was launched at the Bromborough shipyard of McTay Marine on 2 June 1985 and delivered two months later. Power comes from two 6-cylinder Kromhout engines, each of 1360bhp, driving two Schottel directional propellers. This gives her a bollard pull of 34 tonnes. In 2002, the towage operations of Red Funnel were taken over by Adsteam which, as explained in the introduction, was itself taken over by Svitzer. We see her at Southampton on 2 June 2007. Later renamed **Svitzer Bevois**, she transferred to the Bristol Channel in 2008, at first working in South Wales but then moving to the English side and based in Avonmouth.

(BMc)

The **Redbridge** can claim no credit for aesthetic appearance, being possibly one of the least attractive looking tugs of her generation. She was built by the Yorkshire Drydock Company in Hull and floated out of the drydock where she was built on 16 June 1995. She was then towed to Albert Dock in Hull where the superstructure and wheelhouse were added. She was delivered to Red Funnel in late August 1995. The Red Funnel Group had been acquired by Associated British Ports six years earlier and the Group was sold in 2001. Red Funnel Towage was formed that same year but sold in 2002 to Adsteam Marine Ltd. It was a further three years before the **Redbridge** was renamed **Adsteam Redbridge**. She became **Svitzer Redbridge** when Svitzer took over Adsteam in 2007. Her two Kromhout 9-cylinder engines, each of 2053bhp, drive two forward-mounted Voith-Schneider propellers giving her a bollard pull of 45 tonnes. Photographed at Southampton soon after assisting the vehicle carrier **Auto Banner** on 20 September 2005, she left the Solent in mid-February 2011 and has since been based on the River Tyne.

(Chris Jones)

The **Lacanau** was one of three tugs built by Ateliers Duchesne et Bossière at Le Havre in 1959/60. She was launched in 1960 as **M'Sila** but delivered as **Colonel** to Enterprises de Remorquage, de Sauvetage et d'Acconage at Sète. She became **Lacanau** in 1973 following purchase by Union de Remorqueurs de l'Océan at St Nazaire. Ownership was transferred to the Les Abeilles group during the mid-1990s and she became **Marion** after purchase in 1997 by owners in St Barthélemy in the French West Indies. Her 16-cylinder MGO engine of 1249bhp drives a fixed pitch propeller in a steerable Kort nozzle. She has a bollard pull of 16 tonnes. She was noted in Simpson Bay lagoon, Sint Maarten, in April 2013. Seemingly in good external condition, she had possibly been adapted as a houseboat. We see her at La Pallice on 6 August 1994.

(BMc)

The **Abeille No. 23** was the first of a pair of tugs built at the Richard Dunston shipyard in Hessle for the Société de Remorquage et de Sauvetage "Les Abeilles" to whom she was delivered in November 1966. This company can trace its origins back to 1864 when its founder Charles Louis Walter established an office in Le Havre, taking delivery of its first tug, **Abeille 1**, the following year. The company claims to have been the first one to commission a tug for salvage and ocean-going work that was more powerful than standard harbour tugs.

Although the distinctive "Les Abeilles" name has always been retained, the company has been taken over several times during the last fifty years, most recently by the Spanish Boluda Group in 2007. The **Abeille No. 23** was powered by an 8-cylinder Deutz engine as was sister vessel **Abeille No. 24** delivered two years later. Both tugs worked at Le Havre. In July 1995 the **Abeille No. 23** was laid up with surveys overdue. Over two years later, in November 1997 she was sold for demolition by local shipbreakers.

(BMc)

The **Indus** has a rather unusual history. Her original name was **Drydock** and this gives a clue to her early history. She was built by the Wilton-Fijenoord shipyard (Dok- en Werf- Maatschappij Wilton-Fijenoord) at Schiedam, east of Rotterdam. Launched on 28 July 1964, she commenced work at her builder's shipyard some three months later and remained there for two decades. In mid-July 1984, she was acquired by Smit International and was renamed **Smit Azie**. She became **Azie Tug** in November 1988 following sale to Damen Marine Services but this name lasted only 14 months as a sale within the Netherlands saw her become **Indus** in December 1989. In 2008 she was acquired by the rapidly-expanding MTS Group, based in Falmouth, and was renamed **MTS Indus**. When built, she had a 6-cylinder MAN engine of 890bhp which gave her a bollard pull of 11 tonnes. In 2002, however, she was extensively refitted. A bow thruster was added and a new engine was installed, this being a 12-cylinder Caterpillar of 1776bhp. This was geared to a fixed pitch propeller in a nozzle and gave her a bollard pull of 24 tonnes. We see her at Milford Haven on 16 September 2005.

(Chris Jones)

Although correctly classified as tugs, types of vessel often termed "multicat" or "shoalbuster" are proving popular with marine contractors. Photographed in Langton lock, Liverpool, on 31 May 2014 are the **MTS Valour** and **Forth Trojan**. Both were involved in the construction of a new container terminal in the River Mersey named Liverpool 2. The multicat **Forth Trojan** was built at the Damen shipyard in Bergum as **Smit Bever** for Smit Marine Services. Her two 8-cylinder Caterpillar engines with a total output of 1558bhp are geared to two fixed-pitch propellers and give her a bollard pull of 23.5 tonnes. She was bought by Briggs Marine and renamed **Forth Trojan** in mid-2012. It was the Damen yard at Hardinxveld that completed a hull built in Poland and delivered it to a subsidiary company as **DMS Heron** on 2 November 2006. An example of Damen's Shoalbuster 2308 design, the vessel was handed over on 26 November 2006 to the MTS Group and renamed **MTS Valour**. Her two 12-cylinder Caterpillar engines with a total power of 1746bhp are geared to two fixed pitch propellers and give a 21 tonne bollard pull.

(BMc)

The **Smit Bronco** is a multi-purpose pusher tug and was the first of three ordered by Smit Transport Europe from the IHC Holland Merwede shipyard at Sliedrecht in the Netherlands. She was launched on 22 March 2006. Vessels of this design (DMPT 2500) can be used for a wide range of marine operations in sheltered, shallow waters and open sea, including pushing, pulling, buoy handling, dredging support work, anchor handling, ferrying of goods and personnel, and supplying fuel oil and water. The spacious superstructure is above the half-raised forecastle deck forward and large work deck aft. However, it is placed well inboard to prevent it from being damaged when the vessel is moored alongside high objects and rolling, and to create a safe walkway to the fore deck. Her two Caterpillar engines, each of 1014bhp, are geared to fixed pitch propellers, and she has a bollard pull of 27.5 tonnes. We see her in Lyme Bay on 27 February 2007 when she was assisting with salvage work on **MSC Napoli** seen in the distance where her main roles were barge handling and personnel transfer. With a storm clearly imminent, she was about to pick up the crew from a barge and take them to shelter. In mid-2014 she was working on a civil engineering project at Kronshtadt in the Gulf of Finland.

(DMc)

In the introduction, we described the circumstances which saw Smit International's introduction to harbour towage in the UK. Having taken over the Adsteam operation on the River Mersey in 2007, Smit made an immediate decision to upgrade the local fleet and resolved to send two vessels from its building programme. These were a pair of Damen ASD 2810 tugs named **Smit Donau** and **Smit Barbados**, They proved to be ideal for the difficult weather and tidal conditions that can be experienced on the Mersey. The hull of the **Smit Barbados**, seen in the enclosed docks on 31 May 2014, was built at the Damen subsidiary at Galati in Romania with completion at the Damen yard in Gorinchem. She is driven by two 16-cylinder Caterpillar engines, each of 2536bhp, geared to two directional propellers and giving her a 52 tonne bollard pull. Unlike the **Smit Donau**, the **Smit Barbados** is equipped for firefighting with a single monitor.

(BMc)

One of the best locations in the UK to see several tugs assisting a large vessel is Battery Point at Portishead. Fully laden Panamax bulk carriers and tankers approaching Royal Portbury Dock require the services of at least four tugs and sometimes six or even seven. On 22 May 2004, the **Sitacamilla** arrives with a cargo of aviation fuel. With a big draught of 14,29 metres, she requires five tugs and is assisted by **Stackgarth** on her bow, **Svitzer Bristol** and **Svitzer Brunel** alongside, **Westgarth** on her starboard quarter and **Portgarth** at the stern. When ships are passing, members of the general public are always keen to find out about them from the enthusiasts who gather at Battery Point.

(DMc)